Diary of a Circus Performer

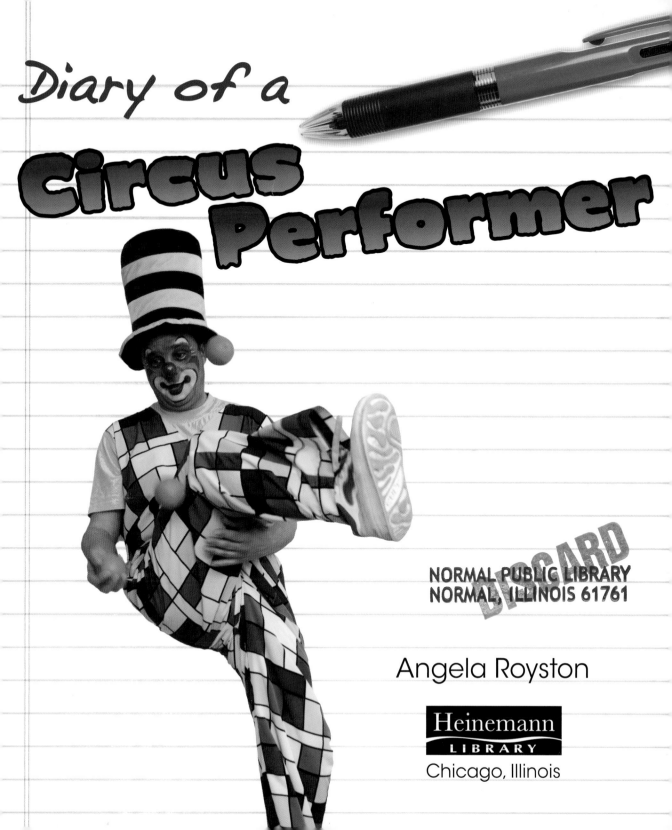

Angela Royston

Heinemann
LIBRARY
Chicago, Illinois

To contact Capstone Global Library, please call 800-747-4992,
or visit our web site www.capstonepub.com

Edited by Daniel Nunn, Rebecca Rissman, and Catherine Veitch
Designed by Cynthia Akiyoshi
Picture research by Ruth Blair
Production by Victoria Fitzgerald
Originated by Capstone Global Library Ltd
Printed in the United States of America in
 North Mankato, Minnesota. 092013 007754RP

17 16 15 14 13
10 9 8 7 6 5 4 3 2 1

Library of Congress Cataloging-in-Publication Data
Royston, Angela, 1945-
  Circus performer / Angela Royston.
     pages cm—(Diary of a. . .)
  Includes bibliographical references and index.
  ISBN 978-1-4329-7580-7 (hb)—ISBN 978-1-4329-7587-6 (pb)
1. Circus performers—Juvenile literature. I. Title.
  GV1817.R69 2014
  791.3092—dc23   2012046857

Acknowledgments
We would like to thank the following for permission to reproduce
photographs: Corbis pp. 7 (© KOEN VAN WEEL/epa), 11 (©
Daniele Leone/Demotix), 12 (© Jessica Rinaldi/Reuters), 13 (©
Neal Preston), 19 (© Bojan Brecelj), 21 (© John Van Hasselt);
Getty Images pp. 6 (Adrian Peacock), 8 (Chip Simons), 14
(Matt Cardy), 15 (Holger Leue), 22 (LEROY Francis), 24 (Jan
Sochor/Latincontent), 26 (Johannes Simon), 27 (Matt Cardy);
iStockphoto p. 20 (© tomazl); Shutterstock pp. title page (© Mira
Arnaudova), contents page (© Pack-Shot), 4 (© CreativeNature.
nl), 5 (© Natursports), 9 (© MANDY GODBEHEAR), 16 (©
Studio DMM Photography, Designs & Art), 23 (© AVAVA), 28
book (© Raulin), 28 pen (© Torsten Lorenz); Superstock pp. 10
(Ton Koene / age footstock), 17 (Marka), 18 (age fotostock), 25
(imagebroker.net).

Background and design features reproduced with permission
of Shutterstock. Cover photograph of Octavio Alegria the juggler
performing during the dress rehearsal of Cirque Du Soleil's
Varekai show at the Royal Albert Hall in London, England, on
January 5, 2008, reproduced with permission of Getty Images
(© Adrian Dennis/AFP).

We would like to thank Paul Murphy for his invaluable help in the
preparation of this book.

Every effort has been made to contact copyright holders of
material reproduced in this book. Any omissions will be rectified
in subsequent printings if notice is given to the publisher.

All the Internet addresses (URLs) given in this book were valid at
the time of going to press. However, due to the dynamic nature
of the Internet, some addresses may have changed, or sites may
have changed or ceased to exist since publication. While the
author and publisher regret any inconvenience this may cause
readers, no responsibility for any such changes can be accepted
by either the author or the publisher.

Some words are shown in bold, **like this**. You can find
out what they mean by looking in the Glossary.

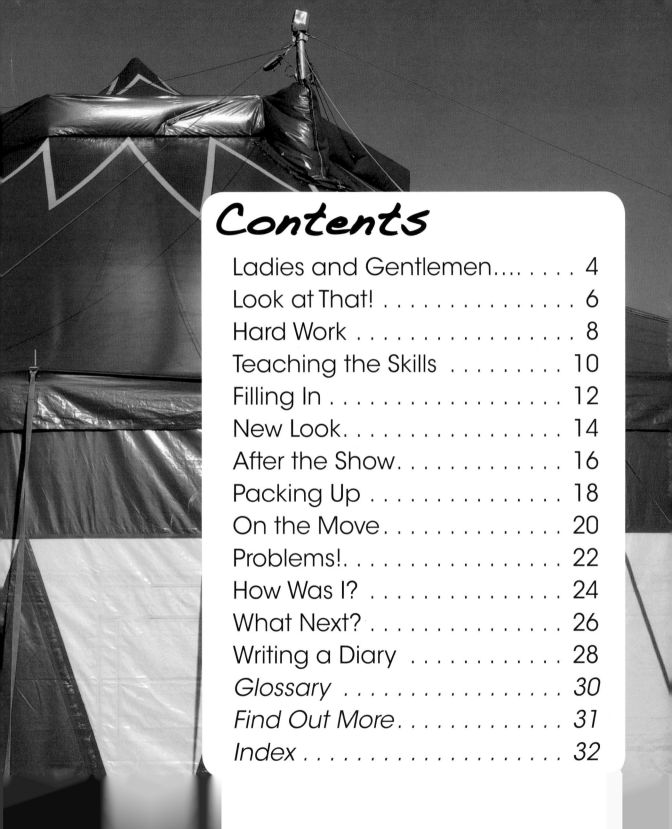

Contents

Ladies and Gentlemen...

I am a circus performer in a small **traveling circus**. I am a **juggler** and an **acrobat**, and this diary tells the story of one week of my life.

Many circuses have a **Big Top** like this one.

I love the circus, and so do the audiences.
I can hear them gasp when I perform, but I
can't see them. I have to keep my eyes on
my juggling!

Look at That!

Saturday, August 20

Saturday is the biggest day of the week for the circus—the day when most people come to see us. This afternoon there were lots of children in the audience.

The ringmaster is in charge. He tells the audience who will perform next.

The **trapeze artists** were breathtaking. They were really high above the ground. The drums rolled while they flew through the air. The children cheered and clapped!

Hard Work

Sunday, August 21

First thing this morning, we all helped to throw away the trash and clean up the site. Then I practiced my juggling, as I do every day.

I wanted to be an **acrobat** when I was a child because I was good at gymnastics. I joined a circus skills class and found I was even better at juggling.

Teaching the Skills

Monday, August 22

Today, I worked with some children who want to learn how to juggle. They started with two balls, and then I got them to try juggling with clubs.

I told them how I got started as a **juggler**. I earned money from entertaining at children's parties. I also entered juggling competitions at festivals.

Filling In

Everyone has to do lots of jobs in a circus. I was taking tickets this afternoon. It's great seeing all the children coming to see the show. They always look very excited!

tightrope walker

This evening I dressed in a **spangled** costume and helped the tightrope walkers. I threw **props** up to them as they balanced on the rope. I had to aim carefully!

New Look

Tuesday, August 23

The ringmaster said my act needed a new look. So I'm going to change it. Today, I designed myself a new costume.

I often work with a partner. We do the act together.

I have also been practicing some new **stunts** for my act. I'm going to mix some acrobatic tricks with the juggling.

After the Show

Tomorrow we move to a new town, so we started to clean up as soon as the show was over. We sold lots of tickets this week, and the owner was very happy!

The clowns were very popular—they always are. They might look like they are just fooling around, but they have to practice a lot!

Packing Up

Wednesday, August 24

Everyone worked together to take down the **Big Top** and pack up all the **wagons**. We're used to doing this, so we worked as fast as we could.

Robanito

Can you guess whom this wagon belongs to?

I helped to fold up the Big Top. It was hard work! Then it was loaded onto a truck. The circus is always on the move. I often miss being at home with my family.

On the Move

We set off to the next town. I drove my **recreational vehicle (RV)** and followed the **wagon** in front. The RV is small, but it's my home!

Putting up the **Big Top** is hard work.

When we arrived, it all began again. We unloaded and started to set up the site. Then we had some food. Now it's late and I'm so tired!

Problems!

Thursday, August 25

Setting up the circus is even harder than packing it up! And today we had an extra problem. The tightrope walker had to go home because her mom was very sick.

The owner told me I had to take over—but not on the **high wire**, thank goodness! He knows I like acrobatics. I stopped what I was doing and started practicing!

How Was I?

I was so nervous before my performance. The music began and I cartwheeled into the ring. I did some **stunts** on the rope ladder and then some balances on metal poles.

Then I started juggling hoops. The audience loved it. Afterward, the owner said I was amazing and very talented. He was right— I saved the show!

What Next?

Friday, August 26

If I am so talented, maybe I should apply to work in a bigger circus! **Cirque du Soleil** is one of the best. If I worked for them, I could get to travel abroad.

This **acrobat** performs in the Cirque du Soleil.

Gerry Cottle's was an old circus that is still famous today.

No, I think I'll stay here for a few more years. I'll practice and improve my skills. People who work together in a circus are like a family. I don't want to leave my circus family yet.

Writing a Diary

You can write a diary, too! Your diary can describe your life—what you saw, what you felt, and the events that happened.

You could write a diary with your friends about an event that you all enjoyed. Each of you writes something about the event. Then read your entries to each other.

Work hard and you might become a star writer one day!

Here are some tips for writing a diary:

- Start each entry with the day and the date. You don't have to include an entry for every day.

- The entries should be in **chronological** order, which means that they follow the order in which events happened.

- Use the past tense when you are writing about something that has already happened.

- Remember that a diary is the writer's story, so use "I" and "my."

Glossary

acrobat person who performs difficult stunts with his or her body, such as balancing on one hand

Big Top very large tent in which a circus performs

chronological in order of time

Cirque du Soleil famous Canadian circus with many acrobats and other performers. The name means "Circus of the Sun."

high wire wire that tightrope walkers use. It is fixed high above the ground.

juggler someone who tosses up and catches several objects after each other

prop object needed for a particular performance

recreational vehicle (RV) vehicle that can include beds, a kitchen, and a living area

spangled covered with small circles of shining metal

stunt act that catches people's attention

trapeze artist circus acrobat who performs on a swing at the top of the Big Top

traveling circus circus that travels from place to place to perform

wagon large trailer or truck. In a circus, seats and other equipment are stored in wagons, and other wagons are used as an office or kitchen, and so on.

Find Out More

Books

Hyland, Tony. *Stunt Performers* (Extreme Jobs). Mankato, Minn.: Smart Apple Media, 2006.

Regan, Lisa. *Circus Performer* (Stage School). New York: Windmill, 2013.

Turnbull, Stephanie. *Circus Skills* (Super Skills). Mankato, Minn.: Black Rabbit, 2012.

Internet sites

Facthound offers a safe, fun way to find Internet sites related to this book. All of the sites on Facthound have been researched by our staff.

Here's all you do:
Visit www.facthound.com
Type in this code: 9781432975807

31

Index